Captured by the Comanches

By Edmee Nyssel Wieden

Library of Congress Catalog Card
Number 92-074788

ISBN 0-927022-10-9

Cover by J. Owen Kinne

Printed in United States of America

CHJ Publishing
1103 West Main
Middleton, Idaho 83644

3031

Agnes Nystel Yates

This book is lovingly dedicated to my Aunt Agnes, Mrs. James B. Yates (Nystel), whose loving care and devotion to her parents was outstanding.

She has helped me a great deal as I have prepared this story for publication.

INTRODUCTION

As a child I sat on my grandfather's knee and listened spellbound as he told me of his childhood, youth and adult years. This was "living history," beginning with the decision of his parents to leave Norway and set out for a strange, new world with plans for a future home. Now Grandfather lies sleeping, awaiting the call of the Lifegiver when He returns to take His faithful children home.

Grandfather told of his capture by the Comanche Indians when he was barely fourteen years old, and how the Lord, in a miraculous manner, spared his life, protected him, and brought him safely home again. He showed me scars, one on his knee where he was shot by an arrow, and another on his shoulder where an Indian kicked him when he attempted to escape.

Grandfather wrote a book, telling of his capture, captivity, and eventual deliverance. He also had a special message for his readers. It read as follows:

"If the perusal of this little work shall cause one poor, sin-burdened soul to pause in reflection and turn to 'seek God and His righteousness,' I shall feel amply repaid for my labor of love.

"May God's richest blessings attend every reader of these pages is my earnest prayer."

I would like to echo this message at this time and pray that Grandfather's story will help someone to prepare for our Heavenly Home.

TABLE OF CONTENTS

Introduction

Illustrations

Part I
Early Childhood --------------------------------17
Capture in Bosque County --------------------25
Traveling with the Comanches----------------31
Captive in a Comanche Village----------------41
Escape --49
Ransomed -------------------------------------53
On the Homeward Trail ----------------------57
Blessings from Ole's Capture------------------65

Part II
Home in Texas ------------------------------69
New Bible Truths and Victory ---------------71
Baptism--------------------------------------77

Epilogue

Bibliography

Brief History of Norse SDA Church

Illustrations and Map

Historical Account

Ole T. Nystel
January 4, 1852 - November 18, 1930
Legendary Hero of the Wild Western Frontier

Terry Nystel
Father of Ole T. Nystel

Ole T. Nystel and his wife, Annie Olena,
standing at the site of his capture by
the Comanche Indians on March 20, 1867.

This is the small church erected
by Ole T. Nystel in Bosque County, Texas.
He is buried here, and his grave site is to have
a marker placed there in commemoration of his
contributions to the State of Texas.

Ole T. Nystel and his wife, Annie Olena,
on their Golden Wedding Anniversary

Ole T. Nystel
On Golden Mountain, site of his capture
by the Comanches, March 20, 1867.

Smokey Hills, Kansas - Ole ransomed from Comanches.

Council Grove - Ole last saw Molly

Mouth of Little Arkansas River - Indian Agent
    reimbursed trader

Approximate route of Homeward Trail, a distance of
    approximately 500 miles, walked by Ole

PART I

Chapter 1

Early Childhood

"Mama, Mama! Make Ole quit teasing me," begged little Annie. "He's pulling my hair again!"

"Stop it at once, Ole," ordered Mama.

Laughing, Ole dropped his sister's braids and scooted around the corner of the barn to the barnyard to try his hand at teasing the stock. On the way he saw big Tabby asleep and tickled the cat's whiskers until he sneezed and opened a reproachful eye. Gus, the dog, was loping along at his heels, so Ole gave him a pat and gently tweaked an ear. Then he vaulted onto the back of a browsing calf, and away they went for a short run around the pasture.

"Ole, Ole!" called Mother, but she received no answer for the moment, for Ole was doing his morning chores and exploring around the farm. Ole was very faithful about his assigned duties and took pride in doing them well. At the Nystel home everyone, young and old, had plenty to do to keep the farm running smoothly.

Little Ole was a busy, happy Norwegian boy living on the wild frontier of Henderson County, Texas in the middle of the eighteenth century.

17

CAPTURED BY THE COMANCHES

That day, as usual, the entire family was very busy. So busy, in fact, that Mother did not have the time to talk and counsel with Ole as she wished, until that evening. And so, after the evening meal and worship, Mother Signe called little Ole to her.

"Son," she said, "you must mend your ways. You must be a good boy or else the devil will get you."

Ole's eyes grew large with fear and wonder at this new thought. He had always been told that the devil had split hooves, a forked tail, fire spewing out of his mouth, and that he carried a pitchfork when he came to claim his own.

Soberly, Ole said, "Mother, I'll be a good boy. I don't want to have any business with him."

Smiling, Mother Signe gave her young son a hug and a kiss, sent him off to bed, and took up her knitting. Seated before the fireplace in the quiet of the evening, she relaxed and began to muse over the past few years of her life, and the many changes the years had wrought.

Signe's thoughts flew to her native land, Norway, a beautiful country with snowy, white mountain peaks, fjords of crystal-clear water rushing along to the sea, and stately evergreen trees. Wistfully, she visualized her native village with her own dear home nestled there among the trees with smoke curling up from the chimney. She recalled the friends and relatives visiting there in Aamili, Prestegjeld, Arndal, Norway before their departure for America.

Signe recalled that in the 1800s many Norwegians began thinking of traveling to the New World, America. Many of them had limited opportunities in their own, small country and had heard so many interesting facts about this new, strange land, that their adventurous spirits were challenged, and they began to make plans to travel. These Norsemen were like the Vikings of old, filled with courage and determination to conquer obstacles in their way and make a new life for themselves and their families.

Signe's father, Salve Knudsen, too was turning longing eyes toward America. The Knudsens had been corresponding with friends already living in Henderson County, Texas who had made the trip and joined the Norwegian community in that area. They learned that their people were welcoming the newer arrivals and were helping them settle and adjust to the new country.

Signe recalled the very day her father startled them by saying, "Well, Mother, it's time we were packing and getting ready for our long trip to the New World. It's hard to leave home and loved ones, but we shall be among friends, and it will be easier to rear our family in America."

"Yes, Papa," said Mama. "I shall begin today, and the youngsters will help me."

Papa left to apply for the visa which would give them permission to travel from Norway to the United States of America.

Signe remembered her courageous mother packing and planning for the long, ocean voyage. That was a time of great decisions for all, decisions of which precious possessions to take and which to leave. All had sacrifices to make. But, considering the promising future of a new home in America, a land of limitless opportunities, they felt any sacrifice was well worth it.

Signe could recall the farewell feast with friends and relatives and the last tearful goodbys - goodbys to many dear ones she would never see again on this earth. She especially remembered one farewell, a sad parting from a certain young man, Terry Nystel. How she had hoped that he, too, would make the trip to America, either then or later.

Signe Knudsen left Norway with her family in June of 1846 with a passport for America. The family boarded a sailing vessel and traveled for seven weeks across the stormy Atlantic Ocean. They had no fear of ocean travel; they just enjoyed the storms, feeling that this added spice to their many adventures.

After seven weeks they arrived at Shrevesport, Louisiana. Here Father Knudsen had arranged to have their household possessions moved to Henderson County, Texas by ox train. The family traveled with this train and arrived at their destination in December, 1846. How happy they were to be greeted by Norwegian friends on arrival, to have a good, warm bed to sleep in again, and delicious Norwegian food to eat. But, best of all was the joy and comfort of being among dear, familiar friends in this new land.

The Knudsens were greeted as family members, and soon plans were underway to help them build a home. The men held a work bee, and the women supplied potluck dinners, while the youngsters ran errands, sampled the food, and did whatever they could to help. The kindness and generosity of these early settlers helped to establish the newcomers and to weld the scattered homes into an organized community, the groundwork for our great country.

Soon the Knudsen family was settled into their new home and the community life, a new and different experience for them. They wrote back to their friends and relatives in Norway, giving them a glowing report of their trip, their safe arrival, and of how happy they all were in Texas. They told them that portions of Texas were similar to Norway, similar in mountains, streams, vegetation, and virgin beauty. They urged their friends to come and join them.

And come they did - in 1849. Ole Tergerson Nystel, living on a farm named Nystel (meaning "new home") had begun to think, talk, and plan for a trip to America. He urged others to join him and his family. As a result, a group from Aamili, Prestegjeld, Arndal, Norway left at the same time. Among them were the Ole Tergerson Nystel family, the Ole Anderson family, and the Berget Tergerson family. This group boarded a sailing vessel for America. However, this trip took all of nine weeks before the weary group reached Shrevesport, Louisiana. Here, they too, moved all personal possessions, traveling by ox train to Henderson County, Texas and settled in the same location at Brownsboro.

Signe recalled how living in the same settlement had helped her and Terry Nystel to become better acquainted. Their friendship had blossomed into romance, and before long, their friends and relatives had a joyous event to celebrate - their wedding in May of 1851.

Then on January 4, 1853, their joy was complete when a sturdy, infant son, Ole T. Nystel, joined their family. How they did enjoy him! Many plans were made for the future of this very special young son of theirs. As Signe would cuddle her small son, crooning Norwegian lullabys to him, it seemed that her cup of joy was filled to overflowing. She prayed that he would grow up to be a faithful son, an honorable man, and a success in life. But she always prayed first and foremost for Divine protection for her little Ole.

CAPTURED BY THE COMANCHES

As time passed by, two small daughters, Toni and Annie, came to join their family. Ole loved his small sisters and enjoyed watching them coo and laugh. But when they cried, he felt it was time for Mother to take over. Many times he would sit or stand and rock the cradle to lull the little babies to sleep, and then tiptoe quietly outside.

Signe yawned, put away her knitting and banked the fire, then went to bed. Another busy day was ahead for her. But first she knelt and thanked her Heavenly Father again for the many blessings He had bestowed upon her. She had a kind, loving husband and a comfortable home, dear children, health, friends and relatives nearby, as well as protection from the elements, and from the savage Indians lurking in the unsettled areas.

In those early frontier days, both husband and wife were busy from early till late, for the majority of them were either farmers or day laborers, working day by day to make a meager living. The average settler had to practice the very strictest economy to survive. However, this was a blessing, for such a way of life developed the stamina necessary to succeed in those early days. These Norwegians would trade labor instead of cash, thus helping one another to survive and to make ends meet. Also, the fellowship enjoyed warmed their hearts, preventing loneliness, and helping make life worth while as they adjusted to America.

Ole's father was a farmer and worked early and late to provide food and clothing for his family, for he had to depend entirely upon his own daily work to provide the barest necessities for survival. As he worked outdoors, Signe was busy in the home, caring for her family.

Ole grew up helping both of his parents. To him it

was great fun, trailing Father and running errands for him. He adored his mother and enjoyed being with her. They made soap together in the great, black kettle outdoors over an open fire. He would stir the creamy, yellow soap until his arms ached, and he wished it were done. They dipped candles, churned butter, cooked meals in the fireplace, and washed dishes together. As a reward, he would enjoy sweet, fresh butter on crusty, home-baked bread, a feast fit for a king.

As Mother Signe busily worked with her spinning wheel, she would tell him stories of faraway Norway and sing many Norwegian songs to him. How thrilling it was to hear stories of the Vikings of old and their trips, but best of all was Mother's account of her own trip across the Atlantic Ocean.

Then one day, Mother became so ill that she could not get out of bed. Father prepared breakfast for the children and went back to Mother's room to care for her. After awhile he came out and called the children to come into her room, telling them she wanted to see all of them immediately.

Quickly and silently the youngsters gathered by her bedside, fearfully looking at one another and their parents for they knew that Mother was very ill.

Mother Signe lay in bed looking at her children, knowing that the time left to her was very short. Her heart overflowed with love for her dear ones. As she thought of their great need, and that she must leave them motherless, her trusting heart turned to her Heavenly Father above. Tenderly she took Ole's hand and whispered that soon now she must leave him, but that they would meet again sometime in the far future. Signe seemed impressed that life would present more problems for her boy than for her daughters, and that some great danger loomed over him. She earnestly pleaded with the Heavenly Father to protect her family and especially guard her little Ole. She asked her husband to carefully instruct Ole in religious truths and to watch over him for her in her absence. Then her eyes closed and all was quiet.

Ole was stunned when Father gently released his hand and folded Mother's over her heart. He told them that she was asleep and at rest. Her work on earth was done. But her pleading prayers had moved the Father of all, and an angel was to guard her son. Psalm 34:7: "The angel of the Lord encampeth round about them that fear Him, and delivereth them."

Ole's mother was twenty-eight years old when she died in 1861. Ole had been very devoted to her and, being only eight years old, could hardly grasp the fact that she was really gone. Missing her loving companionship, he would at times go looking for her; then he would suddenly realize she was no longer with them, and he would run to his father for comfort. Her memory was a comfort to him then; in the years to come it was a mainstay. He always thanked God for a mother who had prayed for him.

After the death of Ole's mother, his father moved the family to Four Mile Prairie, Van Zandt County, Texas where they lived during the Civil War, 1861-1865.

Chapter 2

Capture in Bosque County

While living in Van Zandt County, Ole's father began to dream of moving to Bosque County, an area resembling their native Norway. He also found a step-mother for his children. In 1865 he married an attractive young lady named Gunnar Gran who cared for his little brood in a very loving manner.

Prior to the Civil War some scattered soldiers and Texas Rangers protected the pioneers. During the war these protectors were called away for military operations, leaving the Texans without protection. The Comanches took advantage of the white man's quarrel and came hunting for horses, cows, plunder, captives, and scalps. Fearing the Indian raids, the settlers banded together in small settlements and stockades.

Since there were no funds for military protection during the Reconstruction Period, Bosque County and the surrounding areas remained sparsely settled into the 1880s.

Many Indian tribes were on reservations with the government giving them food and clothing, and a sort of peace had been arranged. Therefore, the government felt that the Indian problem had been solved. However, as time slipped by, it was learned how false this feeling of security was.

No one was safe. The Norwegian people were afraid to move to Bosque County because of the Indian raids. However, all were anxious to leave East Texas where many had been ill with the ague, a type of sometimes-fatal fever.

Bosque County was very similar to Norway except for the marauding Comanche Indians who enjoyed hunting in this area and were determined to keep it unchanged. The Indians enjoyed their four to six hundred miles of private hunting grounds, Comancheria, and welcomed no trespassers.

In 1866, after the close of the Civil War, a group of Norwegian settlers moved to Bosque County. Terry Nystel and his family were in that group. Soon a beautiful site was located, and the family began carving their home from the wilderness.

They all enjoyed living in that beautiful area. With their new mother filling the empty place in their hearts with her special mothering, this new location became a real home. It was fun for all to watch their garden and crops growing and to help in developing their new farm.

One fresh, spring morning, March 20, 1867, breakfast was over, chores done, and Ole had managed to have a good romp with his barnyard playfellows. Corn planting was planned for the day, and Ole always played a big part in the day's work. His father plowed the furrows, and Ole would drop the corn by hand into these furrows, speeding up the planting process and helping in many other ways.

Ole, at 14, was large for his age, handsome and sturdy, with a big smile and cheerful disposition. He was also a very willing and able worker.

Just before they set out for the cornfields, a neighbor, Mr. Carl Quested, drove up with his ox team and wagon. He was on his way to the cedar brakes in the mountains.

"Hello, Neighbor Nystel," called Mr. Quested. "I'm on my way to Golden Mountain to cut down cedar posts for my place, and I thought I'd stop by and see if Ole could go with me and help."

Father Nystel looked at Ole and observing the boy's eagerness, said, " All right, Carl, he can go with you."

Ole was surprised that Father would let him go. But, with a word of thanks, he hopped into the wagon, and they were off to the mountains. As they drove along on that fine spring morning, visiting and at times whistling or singing, neither one had the slightest inkling of what was in store for them in the cedar brakes.

It was about five miles to Golden Mountain where they planned to work. Upon arrival, Mr. Quested told Ole to fasten the oxen and hopped out of the wagon. He walked about fifty feet away and began cutting cedar posts.

As Ole was fastening the oxen, a horrible war whoop rang out. He looked up to see some painted and feathered savages charging straight for him, shooting arrows and brandishing tomahawks. For a split second, Ole thought the devil had come to "claim his own." His conscience smote him as he recalled some naughty boyish pranks and his mother's admonition: "Ole, if you are not good, the devil will get you."

Ole sprinted for his friend but, after only a few steps, he fell to the ground with an arrow through his right knee. As he lay there in a semidaze, he prayed for deliverance, and if not deliverance, for protection and for his very life, promising the Lord that he would be a better boy in the future. An Indian pointed his pistol at him and commanded him to come to him. Ole was not long in obeying, crawling on the ground toward his captor.

Mr. Quested, still clutching his ax, had started to run about the same time as Ole had. At this time they were on a flat plateau of a fairly high mountain. At the left edge of this plateau was a deep canyon with rocky sides filled with brush. Mr. Quested ran along the curving bluff above this canyon while the Indians cut straight across to intercept him, shooting and howling as they ran. One shot hit his right arm. Mr. Quested made a split second decision and leaped out and away from the rocks. Plummeting down, down, down, he landed in soft, feathery cedar trimmings, left piled there by woodcutters. These cushioned his fall, causing only a few, small scratches, cuts, and bruises. He darted off into the cedar brakes, still clutching the large, sharp ax.

An Indian had run down a more sloping side of the bluff and was right at his heels. But, fearing that ax and unable to shoot with any accuracy in the dense cedar brakes, the Indian turned away. Apparently, the Comanches preferred a live boy to an old man's scalp, so they let him go.

Fear lent speed to Mr. Quested's heels. He tore through the brush at a desperate speed for about four miles without stopping. Soon he arrived home, staggering with fatigue, bloody and exhausted, his clothing and shoes ripped to shreds and his feet torn and bleeding.

Mr. Quested staggered into the house, crying, "Help! Spread the alarm! The Comanches took Ole! Call the neighbors! Go for help!"

His daughter, Martha, took in the situation at a glance and ran for her horse, saddled him, and raced off to spread the alarm.

She galloped from home to home, crying, "Help! Help! Spread the news, sound the alarm! The Indians have captured Ole! Gather at our home quickly!"

Bosque County had no telephones in 1867 so this disastrous news was further relayed by friends and neighbors. Soon the pioneers were galloping over to Quested's home to organize for pursuit. These grim men came mounted on their best horses, armed with rifles, and carrying a little food. They were determined to rescue Ole at all costs. They rallied around Father Nystel, trying to comfort him, saying, "Keep up your courage. We hope to have Ole back soon."

This group of men took off at a swift gallop for Golden Mountain to check it over and determine the direction taken by the Comanches. They soon located the trail and having some skillful trackers in their group, followed the trail at a gallop.

Chapter 3

Traveling With the Comanches

After Mr. Quested's escape, the Indians gathered around Ole. Several Indians held him as another one jerked out the arrow. Ole almost fainted from the pain. His captors then took his shirt, gave it to one of the Indians, and gave him Mr. Quested's old overcoat to wear. One Indian took a sharp scalping knife in his hand, grabbed Ole's hair in the other, and ran the knife around the edge of his hair as if starting to scalp him. It was sharp and pricked, but Ole looked at the Indian fearlessly. Seeing no apparent fear, the Indian put the knife away with a grunt.

His captors led Ole over to a nearby campfire where three of their number were boiling horsemeat. A dead horse lay not far from the campsite, and Ole could see that some choice cuts had been selected for their meal. He was offered some of the cooked meat, but he refused. The braves decided not to share the crackers they were also eating; it was nine days before Ole had food of any kind.

Ole now fully realized that he was a helpless captive at the mercy of these Comanches whose mere name struck terror along the frontier. As he looked at them, painted, bedecked with feathers, wolfing their food and staring at him, his heart quailed, and he pleaded for courage and help from above.

After the meal, his captors amused themselves a bit by testing him for tribe membership. This they did by beating him, firing pistols so close to his face that the caps and powder struck him in the face, bruising and burning it so badly that he felt he would be disfigured for life if he were fortunate enough to escape. He seemed to pass these tests so the braves gathered in a group and held a pow-wow concerning Ole. He knew this by the way they kept pointing at him as they talked.

After this council, he was turned over to one brave named Patter-jo-kay who had charge of him on the trip. This Indian was thoughtful, giving him water and helping him on and off the horses when necessary. He never hit Ole once on the entire trip. At times, Ole wondered if his caretaker could possibly be white, but all the colorful warpaint the Indian wore made it impossible to tell. This man spoke bits of broken English.

Ole saw quite a few horses grazing near the camp, and an idea came for possible escape. He thought he might be able to decoy the party down toward the settlement by pointing to the horses and making signs for many horses there. He pointed first at the skinny, old horse he was to ride, then at better horses, and then toward the settlement. But the clever Indians shook their heads and looked at one another as if they understood he was trying to lead them into danger. They shook their heads and rode away with him in their midst.

As they trotted along, Ole was miserable. Seated on

a boney horse without a saddle, he was cold and in great pain from his wounded knee. The party of six Indians avoided the roads and trails, skulking through the brush to avoid being seen. They took a northwesterly course heading home.

After traveling about three miles they suddenly came upon a man named Fine and his son who were out looking for their horses which these same Indians had previously stolen. Startled by the Indians, the two men raced for a large live oak thicket, tied the mules they had been riding, and plunged into the thick brush. Immediately the savages surrounded the thicket and began firing. Both men escaped death for the cautious Indians, fearing possible arms, did not go into the thicket after them. The older man was shot in the arm but both were able to go for help after the Indians moved on. However, they lost their mules, too.

Shortly before sundown the war party saw a black man driving slowly along in a wagon. Seeing no chance of escape, the man ran to the braves, knelt down, and begged for his life. They were about to let him go when a ferocious squaw interrupted saying "No!"

Then the braves stabbed him through the heart and pinned him to the ground with a spear. One of them took a knife and ran it around the edge of the black man's scalp, holding his nose and saying, "Ugh! Ugh!" Then they pointed at Ole's head saying, "Mucha venna, much venna." (very good) One of them pricked him with a sharp pointed knife and looked greedy enough to take his scalp right then.

The Indians commanded Ole to laugh at the cruel treatment of the black man. His sickly attempt to do this apparently satisfied them, and they traveled on.

33

CAPTURED BY THE COMANCHES

Ole tried to keep his self-possession, hoping for rescue. This hope gave him courage. He rode with a prayer in his heart for life and, if this were not to be granted, for a saved soul.

Earlier, one of the group had left the war party, traveling toward Twin Mountain in Hamilton County. When he returned late in the evening Ole saw he had lost an eye. Later Ole learned this happened while the Indian struggled with another Negro in a battle to the death.

As darkness drew on, the Indians made a short halt to await the rising moon. They killed a calf and ate some of the raw meat with the warm blood oozing out. Some was offered to Ole, but he had no stomach for such food. At this time, they took off all Ole's clothing except for the old overcoat. The fresh calf skin was placed on his horse with the raw side up; then his caretaker picked him up and sat him on the horse. The skin was wrapped carefully around Ole's bare feet and legs for protection and warmth.

Meanwhile, Father Nystel and his friends were on the trail of the Indians. These guardians of the frontier were not military men nor rangers, but many of them had served in one or both branches of the service. They were skilled woodsmen, men who could follow a trail at a gallop, switching horses frequently. These men were feared by the Comanches and avoided if at all possible.

During the Reconstruction Period following the Civil War, there were no available funds to protect the frontier and the settlers had organized for their own protection. It was one of these groups of men who were tracking the Comanches to rescue Ole.

Toward evening the Comanches made a routine check on their back trail and found, to their amazement,

34

these woodsmen following the trail with such speed and tenacity that a hasty flight was imperative. As the moon rose, the war party took off at a furious speed. They galloped, dropped to a trot, then galloped again. As one horse tired they switched mounts and traveled on in this way without stopping. The braves were determined to escape with their horses and captive. Each night they traveled, gaining some distance, only to lose it the following day because of some slower horses in the stolen herd. At daybreak their relentless pursuers would again take up the trail, causing fear and consternation. Ole was never off his horse except as he was lifted from one to another.

One night, Ole's friends were so close he could hear them talking; but a knife to his throat let him know that any noise would be his last. A sudden Texas norther blew up that night and, as snow began to fall, the Indians slipped silently away in the darkness like ghosts in the night. The snow completely covered their trail.

The next morning the pioneers looked over an expanse of unbroken snow. They hunted here and there for a trail without success and finally turned sorrowfully toward home. On the return trail, Ole's father continued to pray for the safety of his son. It was heartbreaking for him to be forced to return home with the news that the Comanches had disappeared with Ole.

The fifth evening of Ole's capture he and his captors arrived at a mountain, one that Ole later decided must have been in Stonewall County. (He discussed this in later years with surveyors.) Here the Comanches had hidden camping supplies such as blankets, a tent, guns, ammunition, and some food with kettles for cooking.

Ole was lifted off his horse and the calfskin ripped

loose, taking great hunks of his skin with it, increasing his misery. Even though he could not walk, he was given work to do. He must get wood and water for them. He managed this by crawling along and pushing the wood and water in front of him.

As night drew on, it became very cold and began to sleet and snow. The Indians kicked Ole out of the tent into the snow without a blanket. Ole had only the old overcoat for protection from the cold. He was hungry, cold, exhausted and in pain, alone in that cold, desolate wilderness. Ole prayed to the Lord for help knowing he must have shelter or die.

He noticed the tent was pitched in the lee of the mountain and crawled over, seeking shelter. He pushed some little evergreen bushes to one side, revealing a small opening. He crawled into that cozy, dry shelter and snuggled up against something warm and hairy. Oh! what unbelievable comfort! Thanking his Heavenly Father for shelter, Ole slept.

About 10:00 a.m. the next day Ole was disturbed by loud talking and yelling in camp. He crawled to the opening and looked out just in time to see the last Indian disappearing in the distance. Apparently all the Indians were searching for their captive slave.

Ole crawled out and over into the tent and began to warm his hands and feet at the fire. When the Indians returned and found Ole sitting there, comfortable and warm, they demanded in signs, "Where have you been?"

Seeing that the snow had covered his tracks, Ole pointed heavenward, saying "Great Spirit, great Spirit!"

This greatly disturbed the Indians. They began to jabber, their faces reflecting wonder, fear, and some

36

respect. They seemed to feel that he was under the protection of the Great Spirit. (And truly he was under his Heavenly Father's care.) There were no beatings that morning.

Catching their horses and breaking camp, they prepared to resume their homeward march. Patter-jo-kay carefully mounted Ole on a horse, and they all trotted away at a fast clip. This was their sixth day of travel and poor Ole felt sad and heartbroken as he left home, security, and loved ones farther and farther behind.

Apparently feeling secure from pursuit, the Indians camped again the following night. They wrapped Ole carefully in a blanket near the fire and made him feel welcome. It seemed they were determined to prevent another "ascension."

The next day they were up early and on the march as usual. For a time the savages were kinder to Ole, but their memory was poor, and soon their daily routine was back to normal.

After riding constantly for hours, the group paused to water the horses at a waterhole. Ole was riding a cantankerous old mule which was slow, thirsty, and obstinate. When the Indians prodded it with their spears to get it going again, it refused to budge.

In disgust, one of the Indians drew a pistol and shot it in the head. It dropped into the water, throwing Ole head first into the water and mud. Laughing, they fished him out and slung him onto another mount as if he were a sack of corn. As they traveled on, Ole's overcoat froze, but he was afraid to say a word.

The next afternoon they stopped near a pond. A hungry Indian put Ole to work digging roots with his bare hands from the edge of the pond. The Indian ate the roots as fast as Ole could dig them. The day was very cold and, to Ole, it seemed impossible to keep digging with his half-frozen fingers. In desperation he quit digging and stood up. Angered, the Indian knocked him into the water. Ole dashed out of the water, butted the Indian in the stomach, knocking him flying, and sprinted away. That was the fastest run of his life. The Indian darted after Ole on foot, but shortly gave up, raced back for a horse, and then was able to run down that jack rabbit of a boy.

The Indians seemed awed that a wounded boy could travel at such a speed. They gathered around him and gazed intently at him. It seemed to Ole that they were recalling his recent "ascension" to the Great Spirit.

But Ole suddenly was overwhelmed with a sense of utter loneliness and despair. He felt wretched and forsaken. Here he was, a fourteen year old boy, helpless in the hands of these insensitive natives. Thinking of his parents and their faith in God, Ole knelt down, looked up, and prayed for freedom saying, "Thy will be done, dear Lord."

Immediately a shadow seemed to pass over him and a voice, audible and sweet, said, "Be in peace; you shall be free."

At once Ole was filled with peace. His fears were gone. He stood up and smiled at his captors, thanking God repeatedly for this reassuring promise.

The wild Indians were frightened after hearing that Voice. They shook their heads in amazement as they recalled Ole's seeming ascension, his swift running in spite of a wounded knee, and the Voice from Heaven after Ole's appeal to the Great Spirit. Carefully, they wrapped him in a blanket near the warm fire.

That night as Ole lay by the fire, resting and warm, he thanked God over and over for His precious promise of freedom. Ole's faith was strong now, and he never doubted nor despaired of eventual escape and return home. Ole now planned to watch for any opportunity to escape so that when God opened the way, he would be ready. He knew now that he was under the protection of his Father above, and he thanked Him then and many times throughout his lifetime for that promise of deliverance from the cruel Comanche warriors.

The next morning, the ninth of his captivity, Ole's captors boiled some beef and fed him a little. This was the first food he had eaten since leaving home. His captors were wise enough to feed him only a little at a time, knowing that after his long fast, larger servings would have made him ill. It was several days before Ole had enough to eat. After that, he was able to eat raw meat. The Indians would cut up the liver, pour gall over it, and give it to Ole to eat. Later, he learned that it was considered to be quite a delicacy prepared in this way.

The course of travel was still northwest over the Staked Plains. At noon one day they reached a steep mountain and stopped for lunch. Weary and miserable, Ole sat down near a pile of dry leaves and scooped out a place to rest. In doing so, he saw a large, shiny, metal ball. He picked it up and bit it, making dents with his teeth. It was very heavy. The Indians came over and made him drop it. When they rode away the shiny piece was left lying on the ground. In later years, Ole made no attempt to find it, feeling it was undoubtedly already gone.

Chapter 4

Captive in a Comanche Village

In about three weeks, the home village was reached. Here Ole was welcomed in typical Indian ways as they tested him to see if he were suitable for future tribe membership.

Ole was a brave, sturdy boy and hobbled around uncomplaining, whistling in a cheerful manner and trying to make friends. He managed to either dodge the kicks and blows aimed his way, or else be brave and laugh at the Indians. Laughter worked best of all, completely mystifying the puzzled Comanches.

Ole settled down to make the best of things while hoping, waiting, and watching for a chance to escape. God's promise of freedom in the future buoyed up his spirits, making daily living bearable.

Ole's daily chores were to gather wood, carry water, and help watch the horse herd. He did his work well, winning the Indians' respect. As he grew stronger he was invited to join in the young Indians' games.

Not long after his arrival in camp, Ole was offered a bride. Several maidens were paraded before him, giving him a variety to choose from - tall or short, plump or slender, homely, ugly, or good-looking. One was even very beautiful. But Ole shook his head "No!" to one and all, for he wanted no Indian bride. His refusal did not seem to offend them.

However, there was one maiden, a rather homely girl, who would not take "no" for an answer, and kept pestering him. Ole became desperate as she continually followed him around, and he determined to teach her a lesson. One day down by the river, he suddenly turned on her and gave her a sound thrashing, pulling her hair and throwing sand in her face.

He expected to be punished for this and was amazed when the braves whooped and hollered, jumping up and down and howling with laughter. This ended his bride problem.

Ole's next adventure was "Acting Judge" for a bow and arrow contest. He stood near the target and picked up the arrows. It was such a hot day that the Indians took the old overcoat away from Ole, leaving him no protection from the broiling sun. Ole was soon red, blistered, and miserable. Tiring of this sport, he dropped the arrows and sprinted away, running downhill with all the speed he could muster. A racing Indian caught up and, giving Ole a terrific kick on the shoulder blade, knocked him flat on his face. Then Ole was marched back to finish his job.

Following this exposure to the sun, Ole was very sick. No treatment of any kind was given to his raw, bleeding, and blistered skin. He tried standing to speed the healing process until his legs collapsed. Painful as it was, he slept on only one side until the other side healed, then reversed the process until both sides were healed.

During this healing time, the Comanches ignored

him except for one old squaw who brought him water to drink, patted him tenderly on the head and cried softly in sympathy.

The Comanches had a simple remedy for thinning the vermin population in camp: they moved. Ole never forgot one of their moving bouts. The natives had packed up and were on their way to a new location when great storm clouds began towering up on the horizon. Lightning flashed, thunder crashed, and in the distance could be heard the roaring winds and rain bearing down upon them. Everyone began lashing their horses to a wild speed, hoping to arrive at their new site and make camp before the storm broke.

The villagers had a bear cub with them which they had caught while hunting. On this particular trip, they had tied the cub onto the back of a horse behind the old woman who had befriended Ole. The galloping horse shook up the bear cub, annoying and frightening him. Angrily, the cub dug his claws into the back of the poor horse causing him to jump and squeal. Kicking and bucking, the horse vainly attempted to unseat the cub. Ole felt sorry for this poor old lady who was about to be bucked off. He was on a faster horse so he galloped to the rescue. Overtaking them, he drew his knife and cut the ropes tying the cub to the horse. The cub fell off and the horse calmed down. His friend looked her gratitude. Then the Indians roped the cub and tied it to three trees.

They all stopped here and set up camp. With everyone working swiftly, they managed to get the wigwams set up just in time before the storm struck in all its fury. Torrents of rain came lashing down followed by pelting hail which riddled the older shelters beyond repair. The Indians in the old shelters ran wildly to the wigwams still standing and cowered inside, screeching and wailing for help from the Great Spirit.

The Comanches were brave enough when faced with man or beast, but let nature go on the rampage, and they were the greatest cowards. Ole was amazed at their terror, and they seemed baffled by his courage. He had been in some bad storms in Texas, but that particular one was the worst he experienced, either before or after. When the storm subsided, Ole went outside to check the damage and found hail lying on the ground about four and one-half inches deep.

After this storm, Ole was more accepted in tribal activities. He joined them in hunting, foot races, and in their amusements, feasts, and dances. To dance, they would form a circle. The young bucks and maidens would hold hands and, to the beat of a native drum, they would dance, jumping and jerking swiftly around the circle. Because of his wounded knee, Ole was slower and less adept, but he gamely joined in.

All dancing was done to the rhythmic beat of a native drum. This drum was a hollowed out log with skin stretched over the end.

The Scalp Dance was a special dance. The bucks, dressed in breech clouts, painted and bedecked in feathers, joined hands with the squaws and circled about, jumping and dancing. The bucks intoned a low deep chanting, and the squaws came in with shrill screams of "Yi, yi!" The onlookers joined in from time to time to liven things up. Then some of the bucks waved scalps about, and everyone yelled louder and louder. Suddenly, the blood-curdling Comanche war whoop rang out, making chills run down Ole's spine. He never joined in this particular dance.

44

At times, the Chief had special feasts and honored guests of his own choosing with special invitations to join him. There was one feast Ole never forgot to the day of his death. That was the "great coffee feast." He was the sole, honored guest that day.

The Chief was a very generous soul, insisting that his guests have plenty, and he was the one to decide what that "plenty" was, and also when they were to be excused from the feast.

When Ole arrived for the feast, he found the Chief stirring the contents of a large black kettle. This kettle contained about seven or eight gallons of rich black coffee. The Chief then served Ole a cup consisting of two parts coffee and one part sugar, thoroughly mixed. It didn't take long for poor Ole to get enough, and he begged to be excused. Of course, the Chief would not hear of such, but he did give his permission for Ole to go outside and empty his stomach, with strict instructions to return promptly.

They sat drinking coffee from early in the morning until late in the afternoon, stopping only long enough for Ole to empty his stomach. When the coffee and the sugar were finished, the feast was over. This special feast was an honor Ole never forgot. To the end of his life, it seemed he could smell that coffee.

While living with the Comanches, Ole learned they had a form of tribal government and law. Visitors were to conform to these requirements or else be punished.

One day a strange Indian came into camp and, seeming to take an instant dislike to Ole, began to beat him. The others pulled him off and told him to quit. This did no good for as soon as he was released, he began beating Ole again. Several braves pulled him off Ole again and held him while others went to one side and held a pow-wow. Then the Comanches took the offender, stripped him, tied his hands and feet together, and left him out in the hot sun all day. That night they unfastened the stranger and insisted that he and Ole sleep together. Ole certainly would have chosen someone else to spend with the night with, given a choice. However, this treatment put an end to the mischief, and the stranger never again attempted to harm Ole.

One day the braves took Ole along on a turkey hunt. They had good luck and were returning with quite a few turkeys. Suddenly, they came upon some Kiowa Indians packing to move from one place to another. The Kiowas had a mare packed and ready for travel. The Comanches ran over and grabbed the mare, cut the packs loose, and claimed her as one of their own. Immediately, pandemonium broke loose. The Chiefs arranged to settle this dispute by a bow and arrow battle. They chose twenty men from each tribe and placed them in two long lines about fifty feet apart facing one another. Mounting Ole on a little pony, they made him ride full speed ahead between the lines as the braves began shooting. The arrows flew thick and fast around Ole and the gallant little pony fleeing for their lives. Ole rode with a prayer for protection on his lips. As Ole reached the end of the line, he was forced to turn around and race back through the fray.

Ole rode through the gauntlet five times, and yet neither he nor the pony were so much as nicked by any of those deadly arrows. Ole considered this yet another sign of Divine protection and offered a prayer of thankfulness as he sped along.

After the battle was over, two Comanches and one

Kiowa lay dead, and several others were wounded. The Comanches got the mare they claimed, and the Kiowas were given the pony Ole had ridden. The dead were buried, and the rest shook hands, so to speak, and made up. The strange battle ended in a grand dance, and both Kiowas and Comanches parted on friendly terms.

Ole observed many different strange customs in tribal life. There were definite rules for courtship and marriage. A warrior would make his choice of a bride and visit her father, arranging and later delivering the price he had to pay for his bride. After taking care of all these details, he must then earn his bride by proving his ability to control himself. All night he must lie perfectly still. If the prospective groom moved as much as a single muscle, the hoped-for marriage would not take place. To make certain that he really did earn his bride, two men watched him all night. At regular intervals, the guards would change so that no one would get sleepy and forget to watch the groom. If he failed, he was later given a second chance to redeem himself and win his bride.

Ole learned that the Indians had a strong belief in a Supreme Being, but they served Him in fear, not love. Many times, especially in times of great sorrow, they would pray and attempt to attract the attention of the Great Spirit. One time, for instance, a group of warriors went on a foraging expedition, and out of the group only one man returned. Ole supposed that the remainder had been killed. Some of the women, evidently wives of the dead, began to pray, sitting with outstretched hands, looking Heavenward and jabbering in pitiful tones.

Without flinching in the least, the women cut themselves with knives and broken glass, digging deep gashes in their flesh, causing the blood to spurt and flow. Several even cut off fingers and toes. It seemed almost that they were vying with one another trying to see which one could punish herself the most.

The composure the poor women maintained and the bravery they displayed were remarkable to Ole. It seemed that they felt they were doing penance for some personal sins which they felt must have caused the death of their husbands.

By their actions the poor widows showed that they had a deep belief in a Supreme Being and were attempting to appease Him by personal torture. It saddened Ole to realize that the Comanches didn't know God as a loving Father who wished to spare His children pain and suffering instead of inflicting it. Ole's heart swelled with gratitude that he had the privilege of learning from God's Word of His love for His earthly children.

Ole noticed that while the braves were absolute rulers in their families many times the squaws managed to have their own ways. The braves' treatment of their wives was very harsh and often on a mere whim, the poor women were punished severely.

However, the ladies had a special opportunity to repay some of this cruel treatment. The braves were always smooth-faced and as they did not shave, their eyebrows and whiskers must be plucked out with a crude type of tweezer. Usually the squaws would do this for the braves, and they knew how to prolong the plucking process and would devise their own personal little tortures. Of course, the braves did not dare show weakness by complaining or even hinting that it hurt.

Chapter 5

Escape!

One day after Ole had been with the Indians for some time, they took him along on a visit to a neighboring village. While there he was surprised to see a young, pitiful-looking white girl who was evidently a slave, too. She was busily scraping some pelts and did not look up from her work. As was usual with the slaves, she had no clothing and was covered with bruises, scabs, and sores in various stages of healing.

When the squaws observed Ole watching the girl, one big, fat woman waddled over to her and yelled at her, pointing to the surrounding woods. She quickly scurried away without a backward glance.

After a bit Ole left too but in the opposite direction. He then quickly veered over in the direction taken by the white girl. Soon he located her busily gathering wood. Ole learned that her name was Molly. She was sixteen years old and had been captured near Weatherford, Texas a short time before Ole's capture.

As they were talking the Indians found them together and gave them both a severe beating, warning them never to speak to one another again.

It was quite sometime before they had the opportunity to finish their conversation. At that time Molly told Ole she was going to run away.

"Where to? And where are we?" questioned Ole.

"I'll go east," she replied, " to Kansas."

Later they learned they were already in Kansas.

Just at this moment, the Indians found them again, and again punished them, warning, "No more talking!"

One last time Ole was able to talk for a few minutes with Molly and told her to let him know in some way when she planned to escape. This last time they were found in just a few moments and punished so severely that both felt another meeting would be fatal.

Ole had been promised freedom. He believed in the saying, "The Lord helps those who help themselves," so he was alert for any possible way of escape. However, three months of captivity were to pass before his dream of escape became a reality.

One dark, stormy evening, Ole was resting on an old buffalo robe in one of the tepees when he heard a commotion out in the horse herd. Hoping to impress the Indians with his vigilance, he went out into the storm to investigate. Near the horses he almost bumped into a hazy form.

"Who's there?" he said.

"Molly," a voice whispered. "I'm running away."

"Wait a minute," Ole said. "I'll go with you." And away he dashed to get a bridle. As he neared the tepee, his dash changed to a saunter, and he moved slowly so as not to attract attention. Casually picking up a bridle, he wandered outside again.

When he was out of sight, he raced back to the horse herd. The horses knew Ole so it was simple to make a selection quickly and quietly. Ole chose the fastest race horse in the herd for himself and using a bridle Molly had brought, he chose another good steady horse for her. He then helped Molly mount her horse and quickly vaulting onto his own, they rode away into the darkness.

They traveled all of that dark, blustery night, sloshing along through the rain and mud. Both were thankful for the crashing thunder, the lightning and pouring rain, hoping that their tracks would be obliterated. They prayed that the darkness would shield them and that the noise of the storm would muffle the sound of their travel.

During the wild, stormy night they talked of future plans, of rejoining their respective families and of what a joy it was to leave their captors behind. As they traveled, Ole prayed for help in eluding their captors and regaining their freedom.

As the sun came up, they both began to worry about Ole's horse. It had worn itself out during the night and was very nervous and frightened by the storm and accompanying sounds.

Hearing noises, they looked behind them. Ole's breath caught in his throat. The Indians, coming at a fast gallop, were almost upon them. Sudden, exultant war whoops made Ole's hair stand on end. Seeing that Ole's horse could go no further and that capture was imminent, Molly cried, "Get on with me! Perhaps we can still escape!"

"No!" yelled Ole. "Run for it!" And he whacked her horse with a big stick.

Ole had always been confident of his own eventual escape but he knew that recapture for Molly would be a living hell, with the possibility that her life would end right then.

CAPTURED BY THE COMANCHES

Molly's startled horse jumped and bolted forward. It seemed to pause uncertainly, then with a wild leap it disappeared from view. Ole ran forward in time to see Molly and the horse sinking down, down, down into a deep, swiftly-flowing river that neither of them had been aware of. The horse surfaced and, with Molly clinging like a burr, swam for the opposite shore. The horse climbed out on the bank, and Molly turned and waved at Ole and the frustrated Indians.

The Indians looked at the more than twenty foot drop into the swiftly-flowing river. Shaking their heads, they turned away. Apparently the risk was more than they wanted to attempt just to recapture a run-away squaw.

Now his captors turned on Ole and roughly demanded why he was trying to run away. They were the same Indians who had originally captured him and were quite disgusted with him, and very threatening. Ole began to laugh and laugh. He knew that if he showed any fear he would get a good beating. The Indians were astounded that a captive would laugh at being recaptured. Without abusing him, they took him over to a clear spot, made a fire and cooked a meal. After finishing their food, they held a pow-wow and decided that Ole would probably not make a good Indian anyway. Since Ole was so much trouble, they might as well sell him and get something out of it for all their trouble. They did not want to run the risk of his escaping for good. His captors knew they could get a government ransom by presenting him preferably at a trading post or a government agent. Since the decision was unanimous, they set out at once to locate a trading post.

Chapter 6

Ransomed

After some searching, the party found a safe river crossing and located a trading post run by Mr. Eli Sewell and his hired help. This was located near Smokey Hills, Kansas.

The Indians entered the fort, found the store, and walked in. Standing under the watchful eyes of armed guards, the Indians signaled that they came in peace, led Ole forward, and placed him in front of the astonished trader.

As Ole stood before Mr. Sewell--naked, covered with scars, bruises and wounds, and with a hopeful, pleading look in his eyes--the trader loved him and wanted him for a son. He was anxious to buy Ole, and after much dickering, settled on a purchase price of $250.00. This was to be paid in flour, sugar, tobacco, blankets, brown paper and some money.

Ole was given temporary clothes to cover him and keep him warm until better fitting clothes could be found. He was then turned over to Mrs. Sewell to feed and care for. Seated in the warm, homey kitchen with steaming food and brown, crusty, home-baked bread set before him,

CAPTURED BY THE COMANCHES

Ole bowed his head and gave heartfelt thanks for deliverance and for these compassionate, loving people

After a nourishing meal, Ole was cleaned up. His hair was long and his head had a solid scab that had risen above the hair with lice crawling all over. Mrs. Sewell cut his hair, treated his head for lice, and arranged for him to have a good, sudsy bath. After this, Mr. Sewell dressed him in new, comfortable clothes.

After the Indians were gone, Mr. Sewell and Ole went over to the river where Molly had taken the jump on her horse. They hunted and called for Molly but she had disappeared without a trace.

The trader and his wife, being childless, became quite attached to Ole. They offered to adopt him, teach him the business, and make him their heir. If he didn't care for this offer, they would send him to school and give him a good job in the business. These offers were greatly appreciated. However, Ole was homesick and longing for loved ones and home. He assured them that their home would be his choice if he were homeless.

It took some time and many treatments for Ole's sores to heal. Many times as Mrs Sewell treated them, Ole could feel her tears dropping on his head.

This post where Ole was ransomed, near Smokey Hills, Kansas, was about one hundred and twenty five miles from Council Grove where Mr. Sewell and a partner, Mr. Whittaker, had a store. About three weeks after Ole joined the Sewells in their home, Mr. Sewell took Ole to Council Grove and introduced him to Mr. Whittaker, explaining that he had just recently bought Ole from the Indians.

Then Mr. Whittaker told them that just a short time earlier a young girl had arrived in the town who escaped from the Indians, and she had told them that there was a young boy who had been recaptured. To his great joy, Ole learned that it was Molly, and that she was living in a hotel in a nearby town. Mr. Sewell took him over to see her. When they met again for the first time since their wild ride through the stormy night, they wept on one another's shoulders and thanked God for their escape from the Indians.

Molly told Ole that she had first ridden madly away from the river, fearing pursuit and recapture. Then she hid for a time, hoping they would not attempt to trail her. After that, she hid during the day and rode at night, still hoping to escape recapture. Finally, she was so weak and hungry that she rode into town and begged for food. The horrified townspeople had her arrested for indecent exposure. After jailing her, the sheriff gave her clothing and offered her food.

Molly was so crushed and heartbroken at such a lack of interest and understanding of her predicament that she cried for a long time. Finally, gaining control of herself, she told the sheriff of her capture and escape from the Indians and that she was terrified of recapture and very fearful of Ole's fate.

When the sheriff learned this, he insisted that she eat, then took her to a hotel and rented her a comfortable room. He informed the citizens of Council Grove of Molly's terrifying experiences and of her need of help and compassionate understanding. They all rallied round and helped to provide her with shelter, warm comfortable clothing, and nourishing food. She was placed under the care of a doctor. Ole knew she had been abused and neglected. Molly was hoping that after her health had improved, she could return to her home in Texas and to her family if they were still alive. That was the last time Ole saw Molly. He made several unsuccessful attempts to locate her again. Many times he wondered how she was, hoping that she was in good hands.

Mr. and Mrs. Sewell wanted to keep Ole as their son. They knew that the Indian Agent, Colonel Leavenworth, would help Ole get home if the Agent knew Ole wanted to go home. To prevent this, they moved around quite a bit dodging the Agent, hoping to win Ole's affection and adopt him into the family. During this time of hiding, moving, and dodging, Ole was left here, there, and elsewhere many times for a few days or longer.

At one time he was left at a hotel in Emporia, Kansas. He was given an upstairs room and when he went to his room that night a number of wondering looks were sent his way. Ole thought little of this at the time, thinking they were only remembering his Indian experiences. When Ole blew out the lamp and climbed into bed, he heard a rapping on the wall. He jumped out of bed, walked over to the window, and looked out to see what was causing the noise. He saw a tree limb blowing with the wind and striking the wall at regular intervals. Ole went back to bed and slept well that night.

At breakfast the next morning, Ole was asked how he had slept.

"Just fine," replied Ole.

He was told that the room was haunted and that there were strange noises in that room at night.

Laughing, Ole finished his breakfast, asked for a saw, and said he would take care of Mr. Ghost. Mystified, the landlady followed him upstairs and watched as he cut off the limb hitting the house. After that taming of the ghost, the local people looked at him with a great deal of respect.

Chapter 7

On the Homeward Trail

Ole longed for home and loved ones and determined that some day, some way, he would be there again. The Indian Agent, Colonel Leavenwroth, had heard of Ole but had been told that Ole preferred to remain with the Sewells.

One day the Colonel happened to see Ole and inquired who he was. Someone told him it was Ole, the boy who had recently been ransomed from the Comanche Indians. Upon learning this, the Colonel took Ole aside for a private visit and was astonished to learn that Ole was longing for home, having been informed otherwise. The Colonel promised Ole he would be homeward bound the next day.

Immediately, Colonel Leavenworth contacted Mr. Sewell and told him Ole was anxious to return home. Then all concerned met at the Little Arkansas Post, and here the Agent reimbursed Mr. Sewell for Ole's $250.00 ransom.

Later, it seemed by sheer accident alone, that Ole had seen the Indian Agent. However, Ole felt that he was being guided and watched over by his Heavenly

Father, and that probably it was just the right time for him to be heading for home. After two months of loving care and good food, his health had improved so much that he was strong and healthy and able to make the long trek home.

Provisions were made for Ole to travel with a government ox train carrying valuable supplies for the Indians. The Agent gave Ole $3.00, a blanket, and an Indian bow and arrows worth about $15.00

As the arrangements were being made for Ole's ransom, Mrs. Sewell ran away and hid rather than say goodby. Mr. Sewell, hastily concluding the final arrangements with Colonel Leavenworth, turned and walked quickly away without a backward glance. Ole ran after him and asked him why he had left so quickly. Overcome with sorrow, the poor man sat down, weeping, and whispered that he could not bear to say goodby. Ole gave him a hug and a pat and said he could not endure leaving without telling him how much it had meant to him to be ransomed and cared for in such a kind and loving manner by the Sewells. He explained that if he were homeless, he would have chosen to make his permanent home with them. Then he told how he longed for his own dear father and little sisters and, giving him a loving embrace and a kiss, he left.

At this post, Ole saw the Indians who had captured him. They invited him to their tepee for a friendly pow-wow. Ole had a trusting heart so he went for a visit. He was so thrilled to be returning home that he made the mistake of telling them his good news, but that bit of news did not go over so well. He was given the ultimatum that he must not return to Texas. They would be satisfied if he remained free in Kansas; Kansas was a good state, they said, but Texas was a bad state. They stated that the Texans were mean and would kill. When Ole insisted that he was returning home, they threatened to kill him if he left Kansas.

Ole understood now why they were arguing in this way with him. He became frightened and began to wish he had not trusted them. While a captive, he had learned that these Indians were supposedly "tame" Indians, living on the Reservation, receiving subsidy from the people of Kansas, yet stealing off to pillage and burn on the frontiers of Texas. This they did consistently. Their atrocities - stealing, murdering, torturing, and burning -were well known in Texas. However, Texans didn't realize at that time that so-called "tame" Indians were responsible for all the raids. The Indians who stole off to do this were really renegades and outlaws. Evidently just what they were up to was not known in Kansas either or else it was ignored.

Among themselves, the Indians had boasted that the government was weak, that they fed them in winter, then let them go hunting other times. The Texans, they said, raised horses and cattle for them, and even supplied scalps for them.

"Ha! The white man is weak and foolish," they would boast. "We are the wise and strong ones. Look what we get away with!" And just to prove what they could do, they would give Ole an extra whack or kick. (This occurred during his captivity.)

The Comanches were afraid for Ole to return to Texas and tell his story. They knew it would make the citizens more determined to chase them out of Texas. It would enable the Texans to track the Indians in their flight. Their diversionary tactics would be useless because the Texans would head straight for Kansas. Ole's information would ruin the Indians' summer sport in Texas.

The Indians formed a circle around Ole, glaring in a ferocious manner, and threatened his life if he persisted in returning home. One of the braves grabbed Ole, scuffling with him and, as they fought, the Indian's blanket fell off one shoulder, revealing a hidden knife. The Comanche grabbed his knife and stabbed at Ole. Realizing he was fighting for his very life, Ole grabbed his pistol from his pocket and fired at the Indian's head who turned him loose and ran. The others, amazed to find Ole armed, backed away. Ole ran for his own camp, thankful to be alive. He heard no more from that group of Indians.

After this last encounter with the Indians, Ole left for Texas. He first traveled with the government ox train that carried supplies for the Indians to Fort Washita. He then went along with an ox wagon from the Indian Territory to Sherman, Texas, walking the entire way. He also walked most of the way from Sherman to Milford, Texas. It was a long, hard trip for a youngster who had been through so much. Although he was just fourteen years old and had no supplies and only a limited amount of cash for food, Ole was a willing and able worker. During his long trek he helped the hardy, pioneer men who in turn helped to feed him. Fortunately, there was no Indian trouble on that entire trip.

As Ole trudged along, slowly covering the long dusty miles from Kansas to Texas, the longing for home and loved ones kept him going. His cheerful personality and whistling kept up his own spirits and helped to cheer the other men.

At Milford, Ole became very ill and suddenly dropped

to the ground, unconscious. The men he was traveling with carried him to a hotel, arranged for a room, and called the doctor. The landlady there was very kind and cared for him with the doctor's help. Ole was so ill that he did not regain consciousness for three days. When he finally awakened and opened his eyes, he looked about at the strange room and strange bed and wondered where he was. He tried to get up but sank back, weak and helpless.

Before long, the landlady came bustling in, introducing herself, and told him how long he had been there. She fed him some warm, nourishing broth, and told him he was to stay in bed until the doctor gave him permission to get up. She told him to remain there with her until he was able to continue on his way home. Ole thanked her again and again and promised to mind her.

In about a week, he was able to be up and about and, although weak and wobbly, was feeling fine. One day, he was in the hotel lobby. To his surprise and joy, some friends from Bosque County came in and inquired the directions to Hillsboro, Texas. They were K. and W. Grimland and K. Hanson. When Ole saw them, he ran over to them in spite of his weak and trembly legs and, catching hold of Mr. Grimland to steady himself, offered to show them the way.

The three men stared at Ole dumbfounded, at first unable to speak. Everyone had given Ole up for dead months ago and here he was, popping up so unexpectedly that they could hardly believe their own eyes.

"Ole! Where did you come from?" Mr. Grimland finally asked.

Then Ole began telling them of all that had transpired since his capture. They began visiting and talking in such an excited manner that quite a crowd gathered to listen and question.

After a bit, Ole invited his friends to come in and meet the kind lady who had cared for him, saving his life. After meeting her, the three men arranged to stand surety for his board and medical expenses. The entire sum was $16.00.

After that, his friends changed their plans and set out immediately for Ole's home, telling him how happy his father and family would be to see him safe. As they traveled, they had a wonderful time, visiting and singing praises to the great and good Heavenly Father for His wonderful care over Ole and for bringing him home again.

A short distance from home, they met Ole's father, traveling in great haste. He was in such a rush that he paid no attention to Ole and his friends in the wagon, but kept right on going.

Ole jumped out and ran over to his father's wagon, calling, "Hello, Father!"

His father stared at him, speechless, unable to move. Then, recovering himself, he jumped out and clasped Ole in his arms. Finally, he choked out, "Thanks be to God! For so long we've thought you were dead. I just received word you were sick in Milford and I was on my way to get you. Let's go home, son."

Upon arrival, his surprised family gathered round, giving him such a warm and loving greeting that the tears flowed, and Ole felt that his cup of happiness was filled to the brim and overflowing.

Ole reached home on a Saturday. He was captured on a Saturday and ransomed on a Saturday. To Ole, it seemed a strange coincidence.

Neighbors and friends came to the Nystel home, anxious to welcome Ole home and learn just what had happened to him. These pioneers became highly indignant upon learning that the supposedly "tame" Indians from Kansas were turning into wild Comanches and plaguing Texas like a pestilence.

Mr. Quested came as soon as he heard that Ole had returned. Formerly, he had been a confirmed atheist, but now he clasped Ole in his arms and exclaimed, "Praise God from whom all blessings flow!" Ole was thankful that this good man had been spared and had come to know God.

Chapter 8

Blessings From Ole's Capture

At home, as Ole pondered on his harrowing experiences and the providential care given him, he began to count the blessings associated with the last six months of his life.

1. He had personally become acquainted with God and had learned to trust Him implicitly.

2. Mr. Quested's life had been spared so that he could become acquainted with God.

3. The Texas people could now better protect themselves with the knowledge that these invaders were not wild Indians, but renegades and outlaws from the Kansas Reservation.

Protests to both the Federal Government and the State of Kansas eventually brought results. It helped put a stop to the Indian raids when it was learned that the Indian braves could be called to account for their crimes. The Texans felt that the lives of many people had been spared by Ole's capture and eventual release.

"All things work together for good to them that love the Lord." Romans 8:28

PART II

Covered wagon and ox team of long ago.
The Nystels moved by oxen and covered wagon
to Texas from Louisiana. Supplies for the Indians
were also transported by such conveyances.

Chapter 9

Home in Texas

After reaching home, Ole gave serious thought to the time spent with the Indians. He recalled his many narrow escapes from death and the many instances of God's constant protection. As he did so, a sense of God's goodness filled his heart. In love to others and gratitude to God, he wrote his first book, FROM BONDAGE TO FREEDOM, in the year 1888. He also never tired of telling others of God's constant love and care for him.

From early childhood, his parents and grandparents had impressed him with the privilege and blessings of having a loving Heavenly Father. They emphasized the importance of living a positive life for good and shunning anything questionable.

His frightening experiences with the Indians helped him to realize and to know that he must seek God for himself. He remembered that, in the past, he had not been a real Christian. He remembered the earnest entreaties of his mother, and how she had begged his father prayerfully to watch over her little Ole. His welfare had seemed to be the burden of her last hours. She seemed to feel that he, being a boy, would be exposed to greater dangers than were his sisters. Ole remembered how father had loosened his hands after she had fallen asleep in Jesus. When he was young, her deep interest and love did not affect him very much, but in later years it meant much to him, especially when living with the Indians. The memory of her kind and loving counsel was a great help and encouragement to him every day of his life.

After returning home, Ole was confirmed in the Lutheran Church, and he did try to lead a strict, Christian life. However, life was good, and Ole drifted along. Twelve to fourteen years passed with religious matters being only a minimal part of his life.

Chapter 10

New Bible Truths and Victory

As time passed by, Ole enjoyed a self-satisfied life style with no challenge for the future. But God had other plans for Ole and brought to his attention some religious meetings being conducted near Turkey Creek in Bosque County.

These meetings were being conducted by Elder A. W. Jensen, a Danish minister of the Seventh-day Adventist Church. Elder Jensen had won several converts to the message, some of whom had been very wicked. The amazing character transformation in their lives impressed Ole, and he determined to learn the reasons why.

At this time, John Wilson, a new convert who had become a lay preacher, was conducting meetings at the home of John Erickson, another new convert. Ole went to a meeting. As they began singing a hymn, telling of the swift passing of time and the coming judgment, a deep conviction came upon Ole. He was so affected that he was unable to follow the words of the hymn. The words, "Too late, too late," kept impressing themselves on his mind. Then and there, he determined to listen, learn, and obey.

Ole was determined that he was not going to be a

Seventh-day Adventist. He had preconceived ideas and prejudices and felt that Scripture sustained his beliefs. Because of this, Ole had come to the meeting determined to stand his ground. But the hymn suggested that it might be to his own hurt. The deep earnestness of the others gave him a strong yearning to accept before it was too late. He felt a longing to know God better in a more real and personal way.

The speaker knew the Scriptures well. He made it plain that Christ was a personal Saviour from sin, and that there is no other name under heaven, given among men whereby we might be saved. Act. 4:12. As he continued, it seemed that each Scripture read impressed all with the clarity of the message.

Next he read Hebrews 9:28: "So Christ was once offered to bear the sins of many and to them that look for Him shall He appear the second time without sin unto salvation." This text impressed the hymn again on Ole's mind. Ole wondered why Christ was to appear the second time. Then the speaker read John 14;1-3: "I go to prepare a place for you, and if I go to prepare a place for you, I shall return again for you." This answered Ole's question - the Lord was coming again for His children here on earth. The thought of such personal and definite visits made to this Earth by the Son of God was almost startling to Ole.

The speaker made clear from Scripture that the coming of Jesus the second time was just as certain and personal and visible as the first advent. He showed that the second advent has been the blessed hope of God's people from ages past. He read Paul's words in 1 Thessalonians 4:16, 17: "For the Lord himself shall descend from Heaven with a shout, with the voice of the archangel, and with the trump of God, and the dead in Christ shall rise first. Then we which are alive and remain shall be caught up together with them in the clouds, to meet the Lord in the air, and so shall we ever be with the Lord."

These words brought vividly to Ole's mind the sad parting from his mother. The reassurance that the living and the dead would be "caught up together" made his heart beat faster with the hope of seeing his mother again.

Ole went home with these words ringing in his ears: "And so shall we ever be with the Lord." He loved the Lord and believed in the Bible, the Ten Commandments, and in baptism. He had been reared by good Christian people, but he felt that new light was now shining upon his pathway and that he must follow it. But he hesitated, confused, praying for help and understanding.

As the meetings progressed, Ole took careful notes of the Scriptures presented and studied these at home, praying for understanding of the truths.

Learning that the Sabbath was the seventh day made him almost rebellious. To think that all of his life he had been wrong concerning this matter of the Sabbath was a great surprise and disappointment to him. To keep Sabbath would make him so different from his family, friends and neighbors, that it would, he felt, be quite a cross. He read over and over again the Scriptures presented at the meetings, especially Genesis 2:1-3, Exodus 20:8-11, Ezekiel 20:12, and Matthew 5:17-19.

Baptism, too, was hard to accept when he learned that it was by immersion at the age of accountability. He had been sprinkled and had always believed in the baptism by sprinkling of infants. But he pondered the

Bible verses on this subject with prayer in his heart for
guidance. Scriptures such as Mark 1:10, Mark 16:15,16,
Matthew 28:18-20, and Romans 6:3-6 seemed to agree
with what the men said at the meetings. Still he
hesitated.

Christ's soon coming, however, was greeted with
joy. He received much comfort and instruction from
texts like Matthew 24:14, 31, Acts 1:9-11, and 1
Thessalonians 4:16-18.

Despite Ole's deepening joy in the blessed hope of
Christ's soon return, he was deeply troubled. He
wondered what he must do for himself and his family
and friends. He prayed and discussed this new
knowledge with his wife. They both prayed for help and
direction for the future.

Ole's home was located far out in the cedar brakes,
away from close contact with neighbors and friends. One
evening after the day's work was done, he sat on the
front porch with his wife. Together they talked about
the new truths that had been presented to them.

"What shall we do?" Ole asked. "I know this
wonderful message is from the Lord, but there are so
many things I don't understand."

"We must pray for understanding and strength to
do the right thing," answered his wife. "We have the
children to think of, too."

Both bowed their heads and prayed earnestly for
help in understanding and accepting God's message.
They prayed also for wisdom in telling others this
wonderful news. Even as they were talking and praying,
a stranger riding a gray horse rode up and dismounted.
Seeing the Bible in Ole's hands, he asked what they were
reading. Ole told him about the new, strange truths,

stating that they did not, as yet, fully understand them.

Then the stranger took the Bible and, beginning at the major points puzzling Ole and his wife, presented them so simply, yet so clearly and convincingly, that the two sincere listeners understood each subject as it was explained.

The stranger carefully and simply explained:

1. Christ's soon coming.
2. The mode of His coming.
3. Christ's love for man. Man's duty to tell others of Heaven and the necessary preparation.
4. The Sabbath, a gift from Eden. No change made in God's law.
5. Baptism, the connotation, significance, and mode.

As twilight drew on and Ole grasped these messages, great joy filled his heart. Now he finally understood and was convinced of what he should do in the future.

The stranger turned to 1 Corinthians 15:1-4 and read it: "Moreover, brethren, I declare unto you the gospel...which also ye have received..." Then he emphasized that to believe meant to believe the gospel and that, according to Paul, the essence of the gospel is "the death, burial, and resurrection of Christ."

Then both Ole and his wife believed and understood this new message and were glad. Ole quoted a portion of Psalms 27:6: "Now shall my head be lifted up above my enemies round about me." It made no difference whether his enemies were wild Indians or fallen angels, he was ready to take his stand and rejoice through Christ, in liberation from bondage, both physical and spiritual.

Ole urged the man to stay with them that night but, with a smile, the stranger mounted his horse and said he must go. He rode down the road - and vanished. They sat there amazed. Later they found that no one else had seen this stranger, either then or anytime.

Ole exclaimed, "We have had an angel come and explain our questions and help us in our perplexity. Let us pray and give thanks."

They both bowed before God and poured out their grateful praise.

Now Ole felt that he was ready to accept the new light, but that first he must make preparation for it. He had enjoyed drinking liquor and chewing tobacco for many years, but now he had learned that even his habits of life should be all to the glory of God. "Whether therefore ye eat, or drink, or whatsoever ye do, do all to the glory of God." 1 Corinthians 10:31.

Ole found that the liquor habit was easily finished, but the real battle was with King Nicotine. Many times he threw away his tobacco quid, only later to go and retrieve it.

Finally one day, he said, "Mother, I'm going out to the corn patch and lick this habit. Please pray for me."

But his wife, Annie Olena, left the little ones in the charge of the older children and went with him to the corn patch. For three days and nights they struggled together for victory. They lived on watermelons alone, from the field next to the corn patch, and prayed earnestly for help in overcoming the powerful hold that tobacco had on him.

After three days of struggle, the desire for tobacco left Ole, never to return. The entire family rejoiced with him in overcoming these habits.

Chapter 11

Baptism

Following this victory, Ole was baptized and began keeping God's holy Sabbath day. He now felt that he had been delivered from bondage twice - first, from captivity with the Comanches, and second, from bondage from sin.

Ole now bought a plot of land about two miles from the site of his capture by the Comanche Indians. Here, the members joined in building a small church. They painted it white and furnished it with pews and an organ. The new Seventh-day Adventists now had a Sabbath home where they could enjoy fellowship together from week to week.

As the years went by, Ole never tired of telling others of his capture by the Comanches, eventual release, and then his new-found faith and joy in the message of Christ's soon coming. He took as a personal message the Gospel Commission: "Go ye therefore, and teach all nations...teaching them to observe all things whatsoever I have commanded you: and lo, I am with you alway, even unto the end of the world." Matthew 28: 19, 20.

EPILOGUE

A cemetery is located to one side of the small church in Bosque County. Ole sleeps there now with his faithful wife by his side, both awaiting the call of the Lifegiver. His children and some friends are resting nearby.

The Historical Society of Texas has discussed placing a monument for Ole T. Nystel, giving date of birth, capture by the Indians, and eventual release. At first, plans were to erect this monument at the site of his capture, but later it was decided the site was too secluded, and it would be best to place it beside his grave where more people could visit and give tribute to this brave, legendary hero of the wild Texas frontier.

At present, there are two historical plaques in Texas honoring Ole T. Nystel. One is located about three miles south of Clifton. This monument was erected in Pool Park which subsequently has become private property. On one side of the monument the names of several pioneers are inscribed. On the other side, a plaque is mounted giving the name of Ole T. Nystel with his date of birth, date of capture by the Comanche Indians, and his release for a ransom of $250.00 given by Colonel Leavenworth, the Indian Agent.

The second plaque is in San Antonio. During the Centennial of Fairs of America, a plaque honoring Ole T.

Nystel was placed in the Hall of Cultures. This plaque briefly gives pertinent information concerning Ole and his experiences with the Comanche Indians.

While alive, when he was questioned about his joy and happiness, Grandfather would refer people to the Bible and offer to help them study. He forgot self, and his personal creed is best expressed in the closing message of his book published long ago:

"Yes, God has been good to me. I have tried in these pages to give honor and glory to Him. I love Him because He first loved me. God gave His only begotten Son that I might live eternally. If these pages will serve to bring some lost soul back to the Father's house in peace - bring some poor lost soul now in captivity to the devil and sin - bring him out from his bondage to freedom and light, my purpose shall have been met. In the eternal ages yet to roll, both He and I will be satisfied, and God shall have the glory."

BIBLIOGRAPHY

1. From Bondage to Freedom or Three Months with Wild Indians by Ole T. Nystel, 1930, The College Press, Keene, Texas
2. History of Bosque County by William C. Pool, San Marcus, 1954, Copyright 1954, Sutro Library, San Francisco, CA, California State Library
3. Lost and Found or Three Months with Wild Indians by Ole T. Nystel, 1888 Wilmans Brothers, Book Commercial and Art Printers, Dallas, Texas.
4. The Comanches, Lord of the South Plains, Wallace and Haskell, University of Oklahoma Press, 1952 First Edition by E. Wallace and C. E. Adamson Hoehl, Fulton Memorial College
5. The Early Memories of B. B. Swensen, Temple Telegraph, February 25, 1934   Archives, University of Texas Library
6. The Indians of Texas from Prehistoric to Modern Times by W. W. Newcomb, Jr., University of Texas Press, Austin, Texas 1961. Library of Congress Catalogue Card No. 60 14312
7. The Nystel Family History given to me personally by my grandmother, Mrs. Ole T. Nystel from her own Bible.
8. The Nystel History, compiled by J. P. Nystel in recent years.
9. The Scandinavians by Donald S. Connery, Simon and Schuster, N.Y., N.Y., Rockefeller Center, 630 Fifth Avenue
10. Winning West Texas from the Comanches, A. P. Memorial Library, La Sierra College, Riverside, CA

Brief History of
Norse Seventh-day Adventist Church
and Adjacent Cemetery

September 13, 1886, P. Olson sold one acre for $5.00 to the Seventh-day Adventist Church, Battle Creek, Michigan, General Conference Legal Association. Recorded in Bosque County Deed Records.

December 30, 1891, first burial in cemetery: Benjamin Andrus, son of Ole T. Nystel.

April 23, 1904, A. E. Anderson sold one third of an acre for $1.00 to the same organization. Transaction recorded in Bosque County Deed Records.
This land was probably for the cemetery. These deeds may have been lost in the Battle Creek fire.

At first, the members met in an older building on the property. The present church was built about 1900.

In 1906, this property and church were redeeded to the General Conference of Seventh-day Adventists in Battle Creek, Michigan. This was done probably because of name change.

In those days, there was no Texaco Conference. Apparently, our Denomination forgot this little church. It has been family-maintained through the years.

October 15, 1983, this little white church was repainted inside and out and re-roofed.

With Elder Cyril Miller, President of the Texaco Conference, officiating, it was rededicated.

Cyril Miller, President of Texaco Conference,
preaching in Clifton (Norse) SDA Church
October 15, 1983

Norse SDA Church, 1983. Built around 1900, Bosque
County, Texas. New roof and repainted inside and out.

Interior view of Norse SDA Church, October 15, 1983.
Golden Wedding anniversary picture of Ole and Annie
Nystel. Graduation picture of Edmee Nystel Wieden in
uniform.

Following is the historical entry of Ole T. Nystel in the HISTORY OF BOSQUE COUNTY, TEXAS. Some of the facts conflict with those in my manuscript. I chose, however, to use the facts that came from my grandparents.

Ole T. Nystel
On Golden Mountain, site of his capture
by the Comanches, March 20, 1867.

NYSTEL-NYSTOL

Ole Tergerson Nystel, son of Terje Ole Nystol, and Signe Knudson Nystol, was born January 4, 1853, in Henderson County, Texas, and died November 18, 1930. His grandparents were Ole Terjersen Nystol and Tone Kittelsdatter Nystol, who came from Arendal Norway, on September 9, 1850, accompanied by six of their eight children, sailing on the Brig "Amerika", and arriving at New Orleans, Louisiana on November 7, 1850. The family settled in Henderson County, Texas at a settlement first known as Normandy, and later as Brownsboro. There Terry Ole Nystol and Signe Knudson, daughter of Salva Knudson were married in May 1851. To this union were born Ole Tergerson Nystel, Tone Nystel, and Anne Marie Nystel. Signe Nystel died in 1861, and is buried in Henderson County. Later in the 1860's the family of Ole Tergerson Nystel moved to Van Zandt County, Texas where his father Terge Ole Nystel married Gunnor Grann. The family later moved to Bosque County in 1866.

On March 20, 1867, Ole Tergerson Nystel went with a neighbor Carl Quested to a place on a point of Kay Mountain in Bosque County to cut some cedar posts. There they encountered some Comanche Indians who wounded Ole Nystel and succeeded in capturing him, and carried him with them. Mr. Quested escaped from the Indians and ran home for help. However, the friends and relatives were unable to catch the Indians and Ole Nystel went off into a fearsome captivity, remaining with the Indians for three months before being ransomed near Fort Leavenworth, Kansas, by a kind trader. Ole would have been killed at once if he had been a grown man; however, the Indians took many captives to raise as Indians from childhood. Ole did not become an Indian however, and thus the Indians found it expedient to sell him for ransom. He returned home to his family after three months travel homeward. He later told how he had been forced to endure many trials and hardships while a captive of the Comanches.

Ole Tergerson Nystel married Serena Hoel in 1872; to this union was born one child, Signe Amelia Nystel on February 17, 1874. Serena Hoel Nystel died April 30, 1877, and is buried in Our Saviours Lutheran Cemetery at Norse, Texas. Ole Tergerson Nystel married Annie Olena Anderson on March 6, 1879; Annie Olena Anderson was born October 18, 1855 and died January 13, 1937; a child of Ole Anderson and Berget Tergerson Anderson who came from Arndal, Norway, in 1849 and settled at Brownsboro (Normandy) in Henderson County Texas; this after a voyage of many weeks, and a long trek by foot and by ox team and wagon from Shreveport, Louisiana. Ole Anderson and Berget Tergerson were married January 29, 1862. Later that year, Ole Anderson went into the Confederate Army and served two years. In the fall of 1865, the Andersons moved to Van Zandt County, and lived there until the spring of 1871, when they moved to Bosque County.

To the union of Ole Tergerson Nystel and Annie Olena Anderson Nystel were born ten children: Sina Belinda Nystel, born May 11, 1880, died March 5, 1972; Thomas Carter Nystel, born July 3, 1882, died May 9, 1963; Oscar Albert Nystel, born January 20, 1885, died October 11, 1918; Joseph Phillip Nystel, born May 16, 1887, died May 23, 1977; Benjamin Andrew Nystel, born December 30, 1889, died October 20, 1891; Lizzie Bell Nystel, born June 26, 1892, died June 30, 1972; Agnes Ophelia Nystel, born August 2, 1894, died July 1, 1981; Ruth Magdalene Nystel, born July 20, 1897, died

June 16, 1965; Clara Gertrude Nystel, born May 6, 1900, died August 31, 1904; and an infant son, born and died May 7, 1903.

Ole and Annie Nystel are buried in the Norse Seventh-day Adventist Cemetery, along with several of their children and grandchildren.

In 1890, Ole Tergerson Nystel and family with some forty other families, including his uncle Kittel Nystel, with about 16 men of the party on horseback and the others in a wagon train of 54 wagons, started from near Clifton in Bosque County in June and arrived near Floydada, Texas on August 12, 1890. They lived in dugouts made in the hillside and covered with wagon canvas which was home until the spring of 1892, when the Nystel family moved to a ranch southeast of Floydada.

Land was broken out of sod ground and planted to corn, cotton and other crops. They exchanged cane from the land with the Matador Ranch for firewood, and sold the balance of the cane crop for gold coin.

The cotton crop was the first raised in Floyd County and was picked, covered from the weather, and then hauled to Vernon, Texas, in the spring of 1892 to be ginned. Cotton sacks were brought from Clifton, as there was no cotton duck in Floyd County.

Religious services were held in the settlers' homes until a community brush arbor was erected in July 1891. The settlers moved back to Bosque County in November, 1899. J. P. Nystel, son of Ole T. Nystel, went to school at Harmony rural school in Bosque County, and later to Clifton High School, and on to Tyler Commercial College where he graduated in September 1908. He was later employed by the M-K-T Railway in Walnut Springs, Texas, at the time of his marriage on July 6, 1910 to Matilda Christine Nelson of Cranfils Gap, Texas.

Matilda Nystel, born July 6, 1889, died December 11, 1981, was the daughter of Peder Christian Nelson and Mariane Olson Nelson. The Nystel family later moved to a farm north of Cranfils Gap where J. P. Nystel farmed and taught school at Cranfils Gap until 1921. They moved to Estacado, Texas and then to Colona, Colorado in 1922, and then to Abernathy, Texas in 1923 where J. P. Nystel taught school at each place. He became a real estate broker and royalty dealer in 1925, and remained in this business for the rest of his life. Children born to J. P. Nystel and Matilda C. Nystel were three: Garland Avery Nystel, born August 13, 1911; Merril Evangeline Nystel, born February 4, 1915; and Archie C. Nystel, born October 23, 1919. J. P. Nystel and Matilda C. Nystel are survived by five grandchildren and eight great-grandchildren.

by Archie C. Nystel